The Spiritual Laws of Manifestation

The Spiritual Laws of Manifestation

Will Stickle

CONTENTS

Chapter One

Life Isn't a Battle—It's a Game (But Most People Are Playing It Blind)

Most people think life is a fight. A struggle. A war for survival.

But it's not a battle—it's a game.

And like any game, if you don't know the rules, you lose. Simple as that. The rules aren't hidden. They've been around for thousands of years. You can find them buried in ancient texts, spiritual teachings, and passed down in whispers by people who actually get it. At the core, it's the law of giving and receiving. The idea that what you send out, you get back.

"What you sow, you reap."

Translation: What you put out into the world—in words, in actions, in energy—comes back. Every time.

Hate people? Expect hate back.

Send out love? You'll get it.

Lie, cheat, steal? Life will return the favor with interest.

And if you want to really understand how this game works, you have to start with the most powerful tool you've got: your imagination.

That's not just woo-woo fantasy talk. Your imagination is the engine. It's the paintbrush. It's the program that writes the code your life runs on. Whatever image you hold in your mind long enough eventually shows up in your world.

Think you're doomed? You are.

Visualize a life of power, health, success, and purpose? That's what starts knocking at your door.

I once knew a guy terrified of getting a rare disease. It was so obscure, nobody even knew how to pronounce it—but he obsessed over it, read about it, imagined himself wasting away.

Guess what?

He got it.

Died from it.

The mind doesn't care about what's real—it cares about what's repeated.

So if you want to win at this game, you have to train your imagination like a weapon. Pointed the right way, it delivers everything you could ever want—health, wealth, love, purpose, freedom. But pointed at fear, anger, jealousy, or victim hood? It'll destroy you from the inside out.

The imagination has been called "The Scissors of the Mind." It cuts the patterns, day after day, that show up in your life. And sooner or later, you're forced to live inside the world you've been secretly building in your head.

To use this power right, you've got to know how your mind actually works. Most people don't. They just react.

You've got three parts of your mind to work with:

1. Subconscious – raw power, no direction. Think of it like a nuclear reactor. It doesn't think, it doesn't reason. It just does whatever it's told—usually by your emotions and repeated thoughts.

2. Conscious – this is your daily driver. The surface-level thinker. Most people live entirely in this part, reacting to everything they see. It's limited and easy to trick. It sees only what's in front of it—poverty, sickness, fear, death—and then reinforces those ideas to the subconscious.

3. Superconscious – the master key. The God-level version of you. This part holds the blueprint for your best possible life. The one where you're doing exactly what you were born to do, exactly how you were designed to do it. Most people ignore this part because it feels "too good to be true." But that's the trap.

The Greeks nailed it: Know thyself.

When you understand that your subconscious obeys your thoughts and emotions, and your superconscious holds the map to your best life, the game changes.

Your job is to get out of the fear-ridden conscious mind and start feeding the subconscious only what you want it to build. That's how you win.

Here's a warning: the subconscious doesn't care if your thoughts are stupid. It just obeys. I knew a woman who used to play pretend as a child, always imagining herself as a widow—black clothes, long veil, the whole act. People thought it was cute. Years later, she married a man she deeply loved... and he died not long after. She ended up living the life she imagined. Not because it was fate, but because the image got burned into her subconscious.

So yeah—don't play games with your mind unless you're ready for them to play out in real life.

Now let's talk about people chasing the wrong goals.

Most people don't know what's actually meant for them. They chase what looks shiny. They go after relationships, jobs, or status that they've been told they should want. But if it's not part of their Divine Design, they hit a wall. Even if they "get" what they thought they wanted, it ends up hollow. Or worse, toxic.

I had a woman come to me once, begging me to help her marry a certain man. She was obsessed. Convinced he was her soulmate.

I told her no.

Why?

Because forcing something that isn't yours breaks the laws of the game.

Instead, I helped her focus on attracting the right man—the one who was actually meant for her. Not her fantasy. Her destiny.

That's the difference between playing the game well... and getting played by it.

When something isn't meant for you, no amount of wishing, begging, or forcing is going to make it work. But when it's right? You can't lose it.

I once told a woman who was obsessed with a man—let's call him

A.B.—this exact thing:

"If A.B. is the right man, you can't lose him. And if he's not, you'll receive his equivalent—or better."

She kept seeing A.B. regularly, but the connection never deepened. Then one day she called and said, "You know, A.B. doesn't seem so amazing anymore."

I told her straight: "Then maybe he's not the one. Maybe the right man is still out there."

Sure enough, shortly after, she met someone new. This man didn't hesitate. He saw her, wanted her, and told her all the things she had always wished A.B. would say. She found herself actually happy. And A.B.? Irrelevant.

This is called the Law of Substitution. You don't lose what wasn't yours—you upgrade it. You swap the wrong path for the right one. No loss. No regret. Just alignment.

Jesus laid it out like this:

"Seek first the Kingdom of God and His righteousness, and all these things will be added unto you."

The Kingdom is within. That means your real power is internal. It's not found in chasing people, possessions, or power. It's in tuning in to right ideas, and letting those guide your steps.

Now here's where it gets heavy:

Your words are weapons.

Use them right, they build. Use them wrong, they destroy.

"By your words you are justified, and by your words you are condemned."

I've seen people talk themselves into disaster.

One woman came to me, confused and angry about her life. She was living in poverty, worn down and bitter. But in her past? She'd had money. A beautiful home. A full life. So what happened?

Well, turns out she used to say all the time: "I'm sick of all this—I wish I lived in a trunk." She thought it was just a throwaway phrase.

Now? She was literally living in a trunk.

Another woman, wealthy beyond measure, joked constantly about "getting ready for the poorhouse." Years later, she was scraping by, almost destitute. Her subconscious didn't know she was joking. It took her seriously—and made it real.

This is how the subconscious works: it doesn't have a sense of humor. Say something enough times, with enough emotion, and it locks it in like a command. Your life will follow.

But the good news?

The law cuts both ways.

One summer, a woman came to me flat broke—eight bucks to her name. Worn out, beat down, zero hope. She wanted prosperity, but didn't see how it was even possible. I told her:

"Perfect. Let's bless the eight dollars. Let's multiply them like Jesus multiplied the loaves and fishes."

She blinked.

"Seriously?"

"Seriously," I said. "Every man has the power to bless, to multiply, to heal, and to prosper. Start with what you've got."

She asked what to do next.

I told her: Follow your gut.

"Do you have a hunch about anything?" I asked.

She hesitated. "Actually... yeah. I kind of feel like going home. I've just got enough for the bus."

Now, her home life was full of lack and hardship. Logic would say, "Stay in the city. Find work. Hustle."

But your intuition isn't about logic. It's about truth. It's your direct line to something higher. It doesn't lie.

So I told her, "Then go. Never ignore a hunch."

I spoke these words for her before she left:

"Infinite Spirit, open the way for great abundance for [her name]. She is an irresistible magnet for all that belongs to her by divine right."

And I told her to repeat it to herself constantly.

She went home. Not long after, she reconnected with an old family friend—someone she hadn't seen in years. Through that connection, she received thousands of dollars in the most unexpected way. It changed her life.

She still tells people, "Talk about the woman who had eight dollars and a hunch."

And that's the truth of it:

There's always abundance waiting on your path.

But it shows up through three things: desire, faith, and the spoken word.

You have to act.

You have to believe.

And you have to speak your desires with authority.

Jesus made it clear:

"Ask, and it will be given to you. Seek, and you'll find. Knock, and the door will open."

The key is this: You make the first move.

The universe doesn't chase.

It waits for a command.

"Concerning the works of my hands, command ye me."

Translation?

Speak it. Own it. Move like it's already yours. And everything will start to shift in your favor.

Every wish, every desire—whether you say it out loud or just think it—is a demand on the system. And the system listens. Even if you only whisper a wish once, it goes into motion.

One Easter, I walked past a flower shop and saw rows of perfect rose trees. For a second, I imagined one being carried through my front door—just a mental image. Nothing more.

A few hours later, someone showed up with a rose tree as a gift.

Coincidence?

Not a chance.

You've got more power than you think. And if you're finally ready to stop playing small, it's time to start playing by the real rules.

Here's what happened one Easter.

I saw a rose tree I liked. Visualized it. Just for a second—nothing crazy. Then forgot about it.

Days later, someone brought me a rose tree. I thanked her. Told her it was exactly what I had wanted.

Her response?

"I didn't send you a rose tree. I sent lilies."

Turns out the florist messed up the order. But life didn't.

The rose tree showed up because I had already called it in. That's how this works.

Once you set an intention and remove the resistance, life has to deliver. Maybe not how you expect—but it's coming.

What blocks most people isn't the world. It's not fate, the government, or the economy.

It's doubt and fear. That's it.

If you can learn to want something without worrying about it, your desires show up faster than you think.

But most people don't want—they worry.

They ask and then immediately doubt.

They pray and then panic.

They dream and then fear they're dreaming too big.

Here's the truth: Fear is just faith in reverse.

It's faith in disaster. Faith in failure. Faith in loss.

Jesus nailed it when he said, "Why are you afraid, you of little faith?"

If you're scared, it's not because the world is scary—it's because you're putting your belief in the wrong direction.

Flip it.

The whole purpose of this game is to see your good clearly—to focus on it until it overrides every mental image of lack, fear, sickness, or failure.

You do that by reprogramming your subconscious. Again and again and again.

One man—very successful—told me how he erased fear from his mind in one moment. He saw a sign in a room that said:

"Why worry? It will probably never happen."

That was it. That sentence burned into his subconscious like a permanent software update. Since then, he expects things to go right. And guess what? They do.

Your subconscious is like a silent assistant that takes notes on everything you say and believe. Every sentence, every thought, every sarcastic joke—it's recording all of it. Then it goes to work making it real.

Think of it like an old-school record player. Whatever you record—voice, emotion, cough, hesitation—it plays back exactly. No edits.

So if you don't like the track your life is playing, break the damn record. Here's how:

Say this out loud with conviction:

"I now smash and demolish every untrue record in my subconscious mind. They return to the dust-heap of their native nothingness, because they came from my own vain imaginings. I now make my perfect records through the power within me—the records of Health, Wealth, Love, and perfect Self-Expression."

That right there?

That's the square of life. That's the Game—completed.

And in the next chapters, I'll show you how to use your words to change your conditions—because if you don't understand the power of the word, you're operating with outdated software. You're playing the game with a broken controller.

Never forget this:

"Life and death are in the power of the tongue." (Proverbs 18:21)

The question is—what are you choosing to speak into existence?

Chapter Two

The Law of Prosperity — You Get What You Expect
"Yea, the Almighty shall be thy defense, and thou shalt have plenty of silver."

Here's one of the biggest truths buried in scripture, ignored by most, and feared by those who don't want to give up their victim card:

God is your supply.

Not your job. Not your partner. Not your inheritance. Not the government.

And you can unlock that supply through the most powerful tool you own—your words.

Isaiah said it straight:

"My word shall not return unto me void, but it shall accomplish that which I sent it to do."

In plain terms?

Your words are weapons. Tools. Commands.

They shape your body. They shape your bank account. They shape your reality.

If you don't believe that, you're playing life on hard mode—and you're probably losing.

Let me show you how this works in real time.

A woman came to me in full panic. She was about to get sued for $3,000. The deadline? The 15th.

She had no money, no backup plan, no idea what to do.

I told her: "God is your supply. There's always a supply for every demand."

Then I spoke the word:

"I give thanks that the $3,000 is on its way to her in the right time, in the right way."

But here's the deal—you can't just say it. You have to believe it. And you have to act like it's already done.

The 15th came. No money in hand. She called me, desperate.

I said, "It's Saturday. They're not suing you today. So act rich. Live in the outcome you want, not the one you fear."

She invited me to lunch to stay calm, and I told her, "This is not the time to pinch pennies. Order the expensive lunch. Behave like someone who's already received the money."

Why?

Because Jesus said,

"All things whatsoever ye ask in prayer, believing, ye shall receive."

And most people miss the keyword: believing.

Not begging. Not hoping. Not doubting.

Believing.

The next day, she called again—excited and confused.

She'd told the maid not to let anyone in, but the maid saw someone outside and said, "It's your cousin with the long white beard."

She called him back in, they chatted for a while. As he was leaving, he casually asked, "How are your finances?"

She told him the truth: not great.

He replied, "I'll give you $3,000 on the first of the month."

She was shocked. But also nervous—it wasn't soon enough. She needed the money now.

I told her: "Don't panic. Spirit is never late."

And then I doubled down:

"I give thanks she has received the money on the invisible plane, and that it manifests on time."

The next morning?

Her cousin called and told her to come to his office.

By that afternoon, $3,000 was sitting in her bank account.

That's how the law works.

But you have to get out of your own way.

If you ask for success and prepare for failure, guess what? You'll get failure.

I've seen people sabotage the outcome because their mind is still stuck in fear-mode.

One man asked me to help wipe out a debt.

I spoke the word, but he kept imagining the worst—what he'd say to the guy if he didn't pay the bill.

You can't say one thing and expect results if you're mentally preparing for the opposite.

You don't get what you ask for—you get what you prepare for.

There's a biblical story about three kings who ran out of water in the desert. They went to the prophet Elisha, who said:

"You won't see wind. You won't see rain. But dig the ditches anyway."

That's it. That's the game.

You prepare for the blessing before it shows up.

You dig your ditches. You make room. You speak the word and act like it's already done.

I knew a woman during the worst apartment crisis in New York City. No vacancies anywhere. People were getting priced out left and right. Her friends all told her to give up—"You'll have to store your stuff and move into a hotel."

She told them, "Don't feel sorry for me—I'm a superman. I'll find my apartment."

She didn't ask for permission. She didn't dwell in pity.

She declared:

"Infinite Spirit, open the way for the right apartment."

And that's what she got. Because she knew:

There's a supply for every demand.

She wasn't bound by the so-called "conditions."

She wasn't at the mercy of the market.

She was working from the spiritual level—unconditioned, powerful, and aligned.

And one with God?

That's more than enough. That's majority power.

The woman who needed an apartment—the one who declared she'd find one when nobody else could—almost sabotaged it.

Why?

Because the moment she thought about buying blankets for the new place, the voice of doubt crept in:

"Don't buy them. What if you don't get the apartment? What if you don't need them?"

That's the tempter. The adversarial mind. The old programming that wants to drag you back into fear and lack.

But she shut it down.

She told herself: "Nope. I'm digging my ditches. I'm buying the damn blankets."

And guess what? She got the apartment—out of over 200 applicants. Why? Because she prepared in faith. She acted like she already had it.

Faith without action is dead.

Your life follows your movement. You don't wait until it arrives—you live like it's already yours.

Those blankets? That was spiritual warfare. She won.

It's the same with the story of the three kings in the desert (II Kings). No water. No hope. But the prophet told them: "Dig the ditches." There wasn't a cloud in the sky. No sign of rain. But they dug anyway. And the next morning, the ditches were overflowing.

You move first. The universe follows.

But let's be real—getting into this mindset isn't easy for most people. The moment you reach for something big, your subconscious starts rioting.

That's the "army of aliens" from the Bible—those inner doubts and fears trying to reclaim territory. That's why it feels darkest before the dawn.

When you're about to level up, all your old beliefs come crawling out to fight. That's when you double down. That's when you affirm harder. That's when you give thanks like it's already done.

"Before you even call, I will answer."

Translation: The blessing is already waiting. You just haven't seen it yet. You can only receive what you see yourself receiving.

The Israelites were told they could have all the land they could see.

That still applies. You're only going to receive what fits inside your own mental vision.

Big visions = big lives.

Small vision = small outcomes.

No vision = stuck.

And let me warn you—it's right before the win that failure looks the most certain. That's the final test.

When the Israelites reached the Promised Land, they hesitated.

They said the land was full of giants and they felt like grasshoppers in comparison.

They couldn't move forward—not because of the giants, but because of how they saw themselves.

That's most people.

But when you know how this game works, you don't flinch.

You hold the vision.

You give thanks while still in the fire.

You act like it's already done—even when there's no evidence yet.

Jesus put it this way:

"Don't say, 'four months until the harvest.' Look again. The fields are already ripe."

He wasn't hallucinating. He was operating from a higher dimension—the fourth-dimensional reality where the outcome is already complete.

You need to do the same. Whatever it is—health, money, love, purpose—it already exists. Your job is to bring it through you, not just wait for it to come to you.

I had a client once who needed $50,000. Time was ticking. Investors weren't biting. The bank turned him down. He was panicking.
I asked him, "Did you lose your temper at the bank?"
He said yes.
I said, "Then you lost your power."
Control the self, control the situation.
That's how it works. Don't let frustration cut the cord to your outcome.
I told him: "Go back to the bank. I'll treat it from my end."
Here's the treatment I spoke:
"You are identified in love with the spirit of everyone connected to that bank. Let the divine idea come out of this situation."
He scoffed:
"That's impossible. The bank closes at noon tomorrow. My train gets there at 10. It's too late anyway."
I said, "God doesn't need time. God's never late. Everything is still possible."
He said, "It sounds good when I'm sitting here listening to you. But when I leave, it feels impossible again."
That's most people. They can borrow belief for a moment, but they don't know how to live in it. Fortunately, I wasn't shaken.
A week later, I got a letter:
"You were right. I raised the money. I'll never doubt you again."
When I saw him later, I asked what happened.
He said, "My train was late. I walked into the bank with fifteen minutes to spare. I calmly said, 'I've come for the loan.' They gave it to me—no questions asked."

Here's what you need to take from that:
• Don't talk yourself out of what you've already asked for.
• Don't confuse a delay with denial.

- Don't act like a victim when you're the creator.

You either trust the process or you trust your fear. You don't get both.

Dig your ditches. Buy the blankets. Walk into the bank like the answer's already printed.

And watch what happens.

The man from the last chapter got his loan—just under the wire. Fifteen minutes before the deadline, he walked into the bank and walked out with the money.

What does that tell you?

Infinite Spirit is never late.

But sometimes you are. Not physically—mentally. Emotionally. Spiritually. You lose the thread. You forget who you are.

That's when you need someone in your corner.

The truth is: you won't always be able to hold the vision on your own.

You get too close to your problems. You overthink. You spiral. You stare at the mountain so long you forget it can move.

That's where a true friend, healer, or ally steps in.

Jesus spelled it out:

"If two of you shall agree on earth as touching anything that they shall ask, it shall be done for them..."

Two people locked in unified belief is one of the most powerful spiritual technologies there is.

When your energy falters, you borrow strength from someone whose belief doesn't shake.

When your doubt is screaming, their vision still sees the outcome clear as day.

They're not emotionally tied up in your situation. They're not hypnotized by your fear.

They're objective. Focused. Faithful. And that's why they're effective.

So don't let pride get in the way.

Ask for help.

Not from the people who will coddle your fear—but from those who can hold the vision for you when you can't hold it yourself.

There's no weakness in needing that. There's wisdom in it.

One sharp observer of human behavior once said:

"No man can fail if even one person sees him as successful."

Think about that. Just one person who refuses to waver, who holds the image of you winning, who doesn't flinch when you're drowning in your own uncertainty—that's all it takes.

Many of the greatest men and women in history made it not just because of their own belief—but because someone believed in them when they forgot how.

Sometimes it's a wife. A friend. A mentor. A sibling.

Someone who keeps the flame alive when yours is flickering. Someone who sees the "perfect pattern" and holds it without blinking.

That's the power of vision.

That's the power of agreement.

That's the power of knowing this game isn't always played alone.

Chapter Three

Your Words Are Weapons—Start Using Them Like It

"By your words you are justified, and by your words you are condemned."

If you understand the power of your words, you stop talking loosely. You stop casually agreeing with sickness, bad luck, and failure. You get precise. You get intentional. Because the second a word leaves your mouth, it starts shaping reality.

I knew a man who said all the time:

"I always miss the streetcar. It pulls away just as I get there."

And guess what? It always did.

His daughter, on the other hand, said:

"I always catch the car. It shows up right when I arrive."

And it did. Every time.

They weren't lucky or unlucky. They were each living out the laws they themselves created through their words. That's not superstition—that's mechanics. Mind-body-reality alignment.

Same with people who carry rabbit feet or lucky coins. It's not the object that has power—it's the belief. The subconscious hears, "This thing brings me luck," and then it moves heaven and earth to make sure that belief holds up.

But here's the warning: when you know better, you can't go backward. Once you understand spiritual law, you can't lean on lucky charms. You've upgraded. And if you try to downgrade again, things break.

Two men in one of my classes were doing great financially. Then suddenly everything tanked.

We dug into what changed.

Turns out, they both bought "lucky monkeys." No joke.

Instead of holding to the truth and speaking their prosperity into existence, they started leaning on superstition.

I told them:

"You put your faith in the monkeys instead of the law. Get rid of them—and call on the law of forgiveness."

They threw the monkeys down a coal chute.

And almost instantly, things turned around again.

It's not about tossing every trinket or horseshoe in your house—but you have to know where the power really is. It's in you. Not in an object. If a horseshoe gives you a jolt of faith? Fine. Use it to boost your belief. But never let it replace the Source.

I was walking with a friend one day—she was deep in despair—and out of nowhere, she found a horseshoe on the ground. She lit up. For her, it was a sign. Her energy changed. Her hope turned into faith, and her life followed suit. Not because of the horseshoe, but because her belief clicked on.

That's the difference. The two businessmen leaned on the object. She recognized the power behind it.

I've had my own battles with this.

There was something I associated with disappointment. Every time it happened, I braced for a letdown—and, surprise, the letdown came. Again and again. Until I snapped the cycle with these words:

"There are not two powers. There is only one power—God. Therefore, there are no disappointments. This thing means a happy surprise."

I repeated it. I believed it.

And things shifted.

Suddenly, the same "thing" started bringing breakthroughs instead of setbacks.

Another example: I had a friend who refused to walk under ladders. "Bad luck," she said.

I told her straight:

"If you're afraid of walking under a ladder, you're submitting to the belief that there's more than one power in the world—that there's good and evil. And if you believe in both, you've already given half your life away."

One day, she was at the bank, trying to access her safe deposit box. Right in front of the vault—yep—a ladder. There was no way around it.

She panicked. Turned around. Couldn't go through with it.

Then my words hit her.

She walked back. Decided to face it.

But when she got there... the ladder was gone.

This happens all the time. The moment you're willing to face your fear? It disappears. That's the Law of Nonresistance. Face the lion, and it evaporates.

"Courage contains genius and magic."

Fear attracted the ladder. Her fearlessness made it vanish.

Here's the deal: you are always pulling the strings. You're the puppeteer. The problem is, most people have no idea what their strings are attached to.

Words are vibrational commands. Speak about disease all day, and your body will follow the script. Complain about money, and your wallet will obey. Talk about failure, and life takes notes.

Once you understand the power of the word, you can't afford to talk recklessly. Not ever.

I have a friend who always invites me over for a "good old-fashioned chat." You know what that means? An hour-long dump of complaints, gossip, fear, sickness, and lack.

I tell her, "No thanks. Old-fashioned chats are too expensive. I'll come over when we can have a new-fashioned conversation—one about what we want, not what we don't."

You only have three valid reasons to speak:

To heal. To bless. To prosper.

That's it.

What you say about someone else will be said about you. What you wish for them, you're wishing for yourself.

"Curses, like chickens, come home to roost."

If you wish bad luck on someone? You're stamping a return address on it.

If you bless someone's success? You're planting seeds for your own.

And yes—the body can be healed and renewed by the spoken word and a clear vision.

Every disease has a mental root. You want the body fixed? Fix the soul first. Start with the words. Start with the mind.

Your soul is your subconscious. And if your subconscious is infected with fear, resentment, or self-hate, it needs to be restored—rewired with truth.

That's what "He restoreth my soul" from the 23rd Psalm really means. Your soul (subconscious) gets cleaned out, upgraded, realigned.

The "mystical marriage" is when your subconscious mind finally syncs up with your superconscious mind—when the programmer meets the power source.

That's when your words start to hit with full force. That's when what you say becomes what you live.

That's when "I and the Father are one" stops being poetic and starts being tactical.

At that point, you've tapped into the divine pattern.

You're no longer a confused, powerless little human running on inherited fear—you're operating from the blueprint of the Creator, made in the image and likeness of power itself.

That "image" means imagination. Creation through vision.

Let's be real: almost every form of sickness and failure comes from breaking one basic law—the law of love.

Jesus made it clear:

"Love one another."

That wasn't some Hallmark platitude. It was a direct strategy.

In the Game of Life, love wins every hand.

Love clears the path, crushes resistance, heals disease, and protects your interests better than fear, anger, or aggression ever could.

Here's a real story:

A woman had a severe skin disease. Doctors said it was incurable. She was in the performing arts, so losing her health meant losing everything—income, identity, future.

Then, on opening night of a new show, she crushed it. Standing ovation. Glowing reviews.

She felt on top of the world—until the next day. She was fired.

Why?

Jealous castmate.

She found out he got her cut out of spite. Her body started flooding with rage and hate.

She caught herself and cried out:

"God, don't let me hate that man."

She sat in silence for hours that night. Not raging. Not plotting revenge. Just asking for peace—for herself, for him, for the world.

She did it for three nights straight.

And on the third day, she woke up totally healed.

That's not coincidence. That's what happens when you flood the subconscious with love instead of poison.

Her disease didn't come from germs—it came from hate buried so deep she didn't even know it was running the show. Once she cleaned it out, her body followed.

Here's the brutal truth:

Most of your aches, breakdowns, and chronic issues are just emotions you never dealt with.

- Constant criticism? That's rheumatism in the making.

- Resentment and hate? That's tumors and false growths.
- Fear and bitterness? That's your liver, your eyes, your blood chemistry all starting to malfunction.

Dis-ease is literally a mind that isn't at ease.

I once joked in class, "Don't ask what's the matter with someone—ask who's the matter with them."

It's not the oyster that poisons you—it's the 19 people you've been arguing with all week.

Here's another heavy-hitter:

"A man's enemies shall be those of his own household."

That doesn't mean your family. That means your internal household—your thoughts, your attitudes, your programmed responses.

Your real enemy isn't the competition, the ex, the critic, the boss—it's what lives inside you.

And until you clear that, you'll keep finding "enemies" outside to blame.

This planet? It's in its initiation phase.

The test is love.

Not emotional fluff—spiritual discipline.

Bless those who hurt you. That's the game-changer. That's where the power is.

"Resist not evil. Be not overcome of evil, but overcome evil with good."

Here's the paradox that breaks most people's brains:

Power doesn't resist. Power doesn't push. Power absorbs, transforms, and moves on.

Nothing on Earth can stop a person who's fully nonresistant.

The Chinese knew it long before modern psychology caught up—water is the strongest element because it doesn't resist. It flows around the obstacle. Over time, it wears down stone. It can sweep away cities. But it never fights. It yields—and in that, it wins.

Chapter Four

The Law of Nonresistance — Don't Fight It. Flip It.

Jesus said, "Resist not evil." Why?

Because evil only exists if you buy into it.

Evil is the product of duality thinking—this ancient, programmed belief that there are two powers: good and bad. But there aren't. There's only one: the Source, the Creator, call it God, call it Law, call it Consciousness. Everything else is a misfire of the imagination.

The old story of Adam and Eve eating from "Maya—the tree of illusion"—wasn't about fruit. It was about perception. They began to see duality. They started believing the lie that there could be something other than God.

That's when soul sleep began.

That's when people started living under the hypnosis of collective fear—believing in sickness, lack, sin, and death because everyone around them did.

And as always, what you believe, you create.

Your subconscious doesn't care if it's true or false. It just plays back the program you feed it.

- You feel poor → you live poor.
- You feel sick → your body complies.
- You believe things are rigged against you → they will be.

You don't live in the "real world." You live in the world you've imagined into existence.

Someone always asks, "But what about kids? They don't even know what disease is. Why do they get sick?"

Because they're ultra-sensitive to the thoughts of people around them. Their subconscious minds are wide open—like Wi-Fi networks with no password.

If their parents are fearful, anxious, and always watching for symptoms, the child absorbs it. Then the body plays it out.

One metaphysician said:

"If you don't run your own subconscious mind, someone else will."

And that's exactly what happens. People get run by their spouse's fears, their parent's trauma, the media's hysteria.

You have to lock down your mental space like a fortress. Because your life will always reflect your mental climate.

Here's a brutal truth:

Resistance is Hell.

Resistance puts you in a constant state of friction and torment. You're at war with life, with people, with yourself.

I once met a spiritual teacher who had the best trick I've ever heard.

He used to baptize children. Now? He baptizes events.

Doesn't matter what happens. Good, bad, sideways—he gives it one name:

"Success—in the name of the Father, Son, and Holy Spirit."

That's it. No overanalysis. No panic. He flips the script immediately.

That's nonresistance in action. That's transmutation.

Here's a story that hits this home:

A woman who understood spiritual law needed money. But she kept getting paired in business with a man who radiated poverty. Talked lack. Thought lack. Lived it. And she started to catch his frequency.

She got frustrated. Blamed him for dragging her down. Resisted the whole situation.

Then it hit her—she was doing it wrong. She was fighting the man instead of flipping the energy.

She blessed him. She baptized the whole situation as success.

She said:

"There is only one power—God. So this man must be here for my good, for my prosperity."

Not long after, through that very man, she met someone else who paid her thousands for a service.

And then? The man disappeared from her life without drama. Situation resolved.

That's what happens when you stop resisting and start transmuting.

Say this:

"Every person I meet is a golden link in the chain of my good."

And mean it.

Because every man and woman is just a manifestation of God in motion, waiting for you to allow them into the divine design of your life.

You resist them—you block your own path.

You bless them—you unlock the next step.

It even works at the level of nations.

You want peace? Stop hating your enemies.

Bless the nation. Send goodwill to its people.

You'll strip it of its power to harm.

You don't overcome evil by attacking it.

You overcome evil by refusing to see it as separate from the good—by staying anchored in your own light.

That's the law.

"Resist not evil."

"Be not overcome by evil, but overcome evil with good."

Let's clear something up:

Nonresistance isn't weakness.

It's not being a door-mat.

It's not rolling over and letting life walk all over you.

Used with wisdom, nonresistance is invincible. It neutralizes opposition without a fight.

Water doesn't punch back — it flows, it dissolves, it wears down anything in its path. Over time, it carves canyons and swallows cities.

Nonresistance is power with no tension.

People tell me, "But I don't want to be passive."

I say: "Then don't be stupid. Use nonresistance strategically."

Here's a personal story:

One day I was waiting on an important phone call. I was tense, impatient, irritated. I rejected every other call. I didn't make any outgoing calls either—afraid I might miss the one.

Instead of trusting Divine Timing, I micromanaged the universe. I turned it into a battle.

And guess what?

After an hour of silence, I looked at the phone and realized... the receiver had been off the hook the entire time. I blocked the very thing I was trying to receive.

My anxiety disconnected the line.

I reset my mindset, blessed the situation, and affirmed:

"I cannot lose any call that belongs to me by divine right. I am under grace, not under law."

A friend went out to make the reconnection call. The store was packed, but the owner stopped everything and personally made the call.

Within minutes the phone line was back—and not only did I get the call I'd been waiting for, but another important call came shortly after.

Lesson?

Your ships come in over a calm sea.

If you resist a situation, it sticks.

If you run from it, it chases you.

I once told this to a woman. She said, "That's so true! I ran away from home to escape my critical, domineering mother. And I married my mother all over again. My husband is her."

She hadn't escaped anything. She just changed costumes. The energy stayed the same.

Nonresistance means you stop trying to dodge what's showing up—and start seeing it as a mirror.

"Agree with thine adversary quickly."

That doesn't mean roll over. It means stop resisting. Stop creating friction. See the situation as neutral and bless it. The moment you stop reacting emotionally, the thing collapses.

"None of these things move me."

That affirmation has more power than a thousand arguments.

Here's the hard truth: You're always facing yourself.
- That person you want to fix?
- That boss who triggers you?
- That partner who "won't change"?

They're all you, showing up in different costumes.

People come to me all the time saying, "Can you treat my husband? My brother? My coworker?"

No.

But I'll treat you.

When you change, they'll either change—or leave your life entirely. But either way, the vibration won't stick.

One student of mine was addicted to lying.

She said, "I don't care, I can't get through life without it."

Then one day, she told me, "I know the man I love is lying to me."

I said, "Of course he is. You lie—so someone has to lie to you. And it'll always be the one you most want truth from."

Later, she told me, "I'm cured."

"What did it?" I asked.

"I moved in with someone who lies worse than me."

Sometimes, the fastest cure is seeing your own dysfunction in someone else.

Life's a mirror. You only ever meet yourself.

And here's another trap to watch: Living in the past.
That's not nostalgia — that's a failure pattern. A total violation of spiritual law.
Jesus said:
"Now is the accepted time."
"Now is the day of salvation."
The past? Dead.
The future? Not real yet.
The only moment with power is right now.
Remember Lot's wife? She looked back—and turned into a pillar of salt.
Translation: Look back and you'll freeze. You'll be stuck, lifeless, paralyzed in regret.

One woman came to me at Christmas, miserable.
"Last year was so amazing. I had money. I gave beautiful gifts. This year, I've got nothing."
I told her: "You'll never see money again if you keep living in the rearview mirror."
Start acting like the gifts are coming.
Dig your ditches. Prepare.
She got it. She said, "I know what to do! I'll buy gift wrap, seals, and twine."
That was her act of faith.
She bought them—with no presents to wrap yet.
And right before Christmas? Someone gave her several hundred dollars out of the blue.
The gifts came. Just in time. Because her subconscious got the signal: I'm expecting good.
She didn't hoard. She didn't doubt. She acted.
And the universe delivered.

Live suspended in the moment.

"Look well, therefore, to this Day! Such is the salutation of the Dawn."

Start the day right. Program your subconscious the moment you wake up.

Say this, every morning:

"Thy will be done this day. Today is a day of completion. I give thanks for this perfect day. Miracle shall follow miracle, and wonders shall never cease."

Make that your first breath, your daily calibration.

Live in the now. Expect the best. Speak with power.

And never resist what you're meant to transform.

One morning, I picked up a book and read a single line:

"Look with wonder at that which is before you."

That was it. That was the code for the day.

I repeated it over and over:

"Look with wonder at that which is before you."

No tension. No expectations. Just wonder. Just presence.

By noon, a large sum of money I'd been waiting for—hoping for—showed up.

Right on time. Right on cue.

Because the energy was open, expectant, and aligned.

That's how real affirmations work.

They're not wishful thinking.

They're command codes for the subconscious.

But here's the catch: they only work when they feel true to you.

If you're just repeating phrases with no conviction, you're wasting your breath.

The affirmation has to land. It has to hit your system like truth, not fantasy.

Take this one, for example:

"I have a wonderful work, in a wonderful way. I give wonderful service, for wonderful pay."

That line has changed people's lives.

I gave the first two lines to a student. She added the last two.

Why? Because she knew the work isn't enough—you deserve to get paid. And paid well.

Perfect work deserves perfect compensation.

She sang that affirmation like a song. Repetition with rhythm.

Rhyme drops straight into the subconscious—no resistance, no filter. It sticks.

Not long after, she landed exactly what she declared: wonderful work, in a wonderful way, giving wonderful service—for wonderful pay.

Another student—this time a businessman—tweaked it to suit his world:

"I have a wonderful business, in a wonderful way. I give wonderful service, for wonderful pay."

That very afternoon, he closed a $41,000 deal.

After months of silence—no movement, no results—everything unlocked.

Why? Because he aligned the internal command with external action.

But don't get lazy with affirmations. Don't make vague declarations and expect precision results.

One woman came to me, desperate. She kept repeating: "I want work, I want work, I want work."

And she got it. Tons of work.

But she never got paid.

Why?

Because she never declared compensation. She was specific about the labor—but not the value. The subconscious delivered exactly what she asked for.

Now she knows better. Now she adds:

"Wonderful service—for wonderful pay."

Words matter. Every line must cover the ground.

Here's the big idea:

It is your divine right to have plenty.

Not scraps. Not "just enough."

Plenty.

"His barns shall be full, and his cup shall overflow."

That's not metaphor. That's the original design.

If your life is small, broke, or hollow—it's not because the universe failed. It's because you've built mental barricades around your own prosperity.

You tear those down with belief.

With expectation.

With consistent declarations that reshape your subconscious into alignment with the law of abundance.

You're not meant to grind.

You're meant to express.

To give.

To receive.

To overflow.

That's the standard. That's the goal. That's your real baseline.

Say it. Believe it. Live it.

The Golden Age isn't some utopia in the future. It begins the moment you stop tolerating lack in your mind—and start claiming your birthright.

Chapter Five

Karma, Forgiveness, and the Cost of Getting It Wrong
Life is a boomerang.

Whatever you send out — thought, word, action — is coming back to you. Sooner or later. And usually when you least expect it.

That's the Law of Karma — Sanskrit for "comeback."

"Whatsoever a man soweth, that shall he also reap."

Most people think Karma is cosmic punishment. It's not. It's precision accounting.

You don't get what you wish for, you get what you are — what you broadcast, whether consciously or not.

Here's a real example:

A woman once told me, "I make all my Karma on my aunt. Whatever I say to her, someone says to me."

One day at dinner, she snapped:

"No more talk. I want to eat in peace."

The next day, during a business lunch with someone she wanted to impress, she started talking animatedly. And right in the middle of her pitch, the other woman said:

"No more talk. I want to eat in peace."

That's Karma — fast-track style.

The higher your consciousness, the quicker the return. The more you know, the more responsible you are.

Spiritual Law doesn't give free passes to people who know better. In fact, the more conscious you are, the faster the slap comes if you ignore what you know.

"The fear of the Lord [law] is the beginning of wisdom."

When you read "Lord" in the Bible, try replacing it with "Law." Suddenly, everything gets clearer.

"Vengeance is mine, I will repay, saith the Lord."

Translation: The Law balances the books. Not God.

God sees you as perfect. The Law sees you as exact. It gives you what you put out.

You're only going to rise to the level of what you see yourself as.

You want more power, more wealth, more freedom?

Start seeing yourself in it. Start speaking and acting from that place before the external matches.

"Nothing ever happens without an onlooker."

Your reality begins in your imagination. If you see yourself failing, the outer world will make sure it happens. If you see yourself winning, the same rule applies.

Here's another story with heavy consequences:

A woman had a strong personal will. She fixated on a house that wasn't hers — visualized herself living there, day in and day out. Eventually, the man who owned it died, and she moved in.

Later, after learning spiritual law, she came to me and asked, "Did I cause his death?"

I said:

"Yes. Your desire was that strong. You forced it."

She didn't murder him — but she set a force in motion. The result? She lost her husband — the man she loved most — shortly afterward.

And the house? A nightmare. Maintenance problems, constant stress, total burden.

That's how the law works. She got the house — but she paid for it. And paid big.

If she'd gone to Infinite Intelligence and said:

"Give me the right house by divine right — one as good or better than this"...

She would've gotten what she actually wanted — without the grief, the loss, or the bad Karma.

Here's the rule:

Desire is dangerous unless it's aligned with truth.

It's a loaded gun. You don't fire it unless you're ready to deal with what comes back.

Anything forced into reality through ego, fear, or personal will is always ill-gotten.

And what's ill-gotten? Never ends well.

It's the root of the phrase: bad success.

Instead, your power move is this:

"If it's mine by divine right, I can't lose it. If it's not, give me its equivalent."

That posture is freedom. You stay open. You stay fluid. You get better than you imagined — without burning down your life to get it.

The second you surrender your ego's script, the universe gets to work on your behalf.

"My will be done, not thine."

And guess what? That's when you actually get what you wanted all along.

The Law of Forgiveness is the emergency brake in this system.

It allows you to stop the momentum of bad Karma before it crashes.

You made a mistake? You spoke wrong? You acted from fear or hate or envy? Forgive — fast.

Forgiveness isn't weakness. It's a reset button.

It tells the Law:

"I understand. I take responsibility. I release this energy now."

And the system responds.

So here's the takeaway:
- You can't cheat the Law.
- You can't game the system with willpower alone.
- And you can't take what isn't yours and expect it not to cost you.

But when you align your desires, ask the right way, release attachment, and forgive yourself and others — the Law becomes your servant.

"Stand ye still and see the salvation of the Lord [Law]."

And that's exactly what you'll get.

Trying to control life through force or fear is a losing game. Every time.

A woman once came to me, panicked. Her daughter was planning a dangerous trip, and no matter what the mother said—lectures, warnings, outright forbidding—it just made the daughter dig in harder.

The mother thought she was protecting her. In reality, she was doing two things wrong:

1. Forcing her personal will onto someone else (a violation of spiritual law), and

2. Feeding the very outcome she feared.

Fear attracts the thing feared. Resistance fuels it.

I told her:

"Take your mental hands off the situation. You don't own her fate."

Then I gave her this:

"I put this situation in the hands of Infinite Love and Wisdom. If this trip is in the divine plan, I bless it and release all resistance. If not, I give thanks that it is now dissolved and removed."

A few days later, her daughter said:

"Mom, I've decided not to go."

Game over. Peace restored. The energy returned to its "native nothing-ness." Because she let go—and let the law work.

It's the same with money, health, relationships—you can't fight your way into alignment. You have to stand still, trust, and let the Law reorganize reality on your behalf.

Here's another example.

A woman came to me upset. She'd been handed a fake $20 bill by her bank. She was sure they'd never believe her or make it right.

I asked her, "Why do you think you attracted that?"

After a pause, she said:

"Oh my God—I mailed someone a bunch of fake stage money last week as a joke."

Exactly. The Law doesn't understand jokes. It understands vibration. She sent out false value and received it back.

We called on the Law of Forgiveness:

"Infinite Spirit, we call on the Law of Forgiveness. She is under grace, not under law. This $20 belongs to her by divine right, and she cannot lose what is hers."

She returned to the bank fearlessly. They apologized, handed her a real bill, and treated her with respect.

That's the power of understanding the Law. You can cancel your mistakes if you act fast and correct your thinking.

Want abundance? Want success?

You have to match it internally first.

Another woman came to me for financial help. She wanted prosperity, but her house was in chaos. Cluttered, dusty, disorganized. No flow.

I told her flat out:

"You'll never be rich with a burnt match stuck in the pincushion. Order is heaven's first law."

If you want wealth, live like someone who respects their environment. Wealthy people are ordered. They're precise. They value aesthetics and flow.

She laughed—but got to work. Cleaned up her home. Rearranged furniture. Organized drawers. Aligned her outer world to reflect her inner intention.

Result?

She received a large financial gift from a relative within weeks.

Prosperity doesn't show up in chaos. The external reflects the internal—always.

Here's what most people don't realize:

Gifts, purchases, and generosity are investments in your future.

Saving from fear is not wisdom—it's spiritual stagnation.

"There is that scattereth and yet increaseth; and there is that withholdeth more than is meet, and it tendeth to poverty."

In other words: Some people give freely and grow richer. Others hoard out of fear and get poorer anyway.

I knew a man who wanted a luxury overcoat—fur-lined, high-end. He only had $700 to his name, and the coat was $500. Logic said: no way.

But he didn't listen to logic. He listened to intuition.

He said to his wife:

"If I buy this coat, I'll make a ton of money."

She agreed, cautiously. He bought it.

One month later? He closed a $10,000 commission deal.

Why? Because the coat made him feel rich. It reset his frequency. He wasn't spending money—he was signaling wealth. And the universe mirrored that.

Ignore that inner nudge to spend wisely, or give generously—and the money will leave anyway. In boring, annoying, or painful ways.

A woman once told me that she had money for Thanksgiving dinner, but decided to "save" it. Skipped the celebration.

A few days later, someone stole the exact amount from her dresser drawer.

The Law doesn't tolerate fear-based withholding.

Spend fearlessly—with wisdom. Give when prompted. Follow the inner impulse to act, even when it seems irrational.

Because when you act in faith, you align with flow.

A student of mine was shopping with her young nephew. He begged for a toy. She said no—told him she couldn't afford it.

And then it hit her.

She realized she was speaking lack. She was rejecting abundance in real time. She was denying her Source. She was forgetting that God is supply.

So she stopped the nonsense. She bought the toy.

And on the way home?

She found the exact amount of money she'd just spent—lying on the street.

That's how the Law works when you're in alignment.

Man's supply is inexhaustible when he fully trusts.

But faith comes first. That's the entry point. Not proof. Not logic.

"According to your faith be it unto you."

You don't get what you deserve. You don't get what you've earned.

You get what you believe is possible.

"Faith is the substance of things hoped for, the evidence of things not seen."

In other words, faith is the thing—it holds the vision. It sustains the idea. It dissolves every negative picture until only the desired result remains.

You don't wait for results before believing. You believe, and the results come.

And if you stay the course—if you don't flinch—

"In due season, we shall reap, if we faint not."

Here's the real breakthrough:

Jesus Christ didn't just teach about karma—He taught how to beat it.

That's what grace is. Grace transcends cause and effect.

Karma is what you earn. Grace is what you're given.

Christ came with the blueprint for getting off the hamster wheel of consequence.

He said:

"You're not under law. You're under grace."

"You will reap where you have not sown."

In other words, God's gifts don't follow man's math. You don't have to balance the books. You can be free.

This state—this grace—is what happens when you rise above the world's programming.

The "world thought" is what you inherited: sin, sickness, death. Scarcity. Shame. Aging. Limitations. The death cult of "realism."

Jesus said:

"I have overcome the world."

And so can you.

He wasn't denying suffering existed. He was denying its final authority.

He said:

"Sickness and sorrow will pass away."

"Death itself—the last enemy—shall be overcome."

And here's the kicker:

Modern science is beginning to confirm it.

Death, disease, aging—these aren't fixed. They're coded into the subconscious, and the subconscious does what it's told. It has no judgment. No filter. It obeys the program.

You believe you're dying slowly? Your body complies.

You believe in eternal youth, renewal, and energy? Your body adjusts.

"The subconscious is power without direction."

But plug it into the superconscious—your divine connection, the Christ within—and everything changes.

Resurrection isn't some future fantasy. It's a present process.

You can be transformed.

You don't have to throw the body away at the end of life. You can evolve it.

Walt Whitman called it the "body electric."

Jesus lived it.

The tomb was empty.

This is what Christianity was meant to be:
Not guilt.
Not suffering.
Not fear.
Freedom. Forgiveness. Power. Life without end.
And it starts with one thing:
Faith in a Source bigger than karma, deeper than logic, and strong enough to break every worldly rule.

6

Chapter Six

C asting the Burden — Getting Out of the Way
     Most people never get results because they keep trying to solve problems with the wrong part of their mind.

They intellectualize, stress, plan, panic — and then wonder why nothing moves.

They're using the reasoning mind, which is full of fear, limitation, and doubt. It's like trying to lift a boulder with a plastic spoon.

The subconscious — your power center — won't respond to weak signals. It responds to certainty.

So the trick is to bypass the intellect and go straight to the real operator: the superconscious — the divine intelligence within.

The fastest way to do that?

Cast the burden.

Let's get one thing straight:

Carrying a burden is a violation of spiritual law.

A burden is any thought that drags you down — fear, lack, resentment, confusion. The longer you carry it, the more damage it does. Not just in your mind, but in your body, your relationships, your finances. It bleeds into everything.

Jesus said:

"My yoke is easy, and my burden is light."

Because He wasn't operating under the weight of this world. He transcended the vibration of resistance — tapped into the fourth-dimensional realm where things don't struggle into being... they just are.

You're told again and again in Scripture:

"Cast thy burden upon the Lord."

"Stand still and see the salvation of the Lord."

"The battle is not yours, but God's."

Translation?

Stop trying to control it. Get your energy out of the way.

Here's how it works in real life.

A woman came to me, panicked over money. She needed it badly. She was tense, worried, blocked.

I told her to repeat:

"I cast this burden of lack on the Christ within, and I go free to have plenty."

Simple. Direct. Specific.

She wasn't "hoping." She was handing it over to the part of her that knows what to do. The superconscious.

What happened?

The belief in lack dissolved. And with it came an avalanche of supply.

Another story:

One student had just received a brand-new piano, but had no space for it. The old piano was still in the studio, and no one to take it.

She repeated the affirmation:

"I cast this burden on the Christ within, and I go free."

Minutes later, the phone rang. A friend asked to rent the old piano.

It was moved out just before the new one arrived.

That's how fast things can shift when you stop trying to force solutions and start aligning with them.

It works on emotional blocks too.

One woman had been tormented by resentment for years. Bitterness had built up and was eating her alive. She couldn't move forward.

Couldn't feel joy.

I gave her this line:

"I cast this burden of resentment on the Christ within, and I go free — to be loving, harmonious, and happy."

She repeated it over and over.

And something broke.

Her subconscious — once poisoned with anger — was flooded with love. Her entire emotional field changed. Her life opened up. She walked out of prison — a prison she'd built herself.

But here's the key:

You don't just say it once. You hammer it in.

Speak it aloud. Say it silently. Whisper it under your breath all day if you have to.

"I cast this burden on the Christ within, and I go free."

You're winding up your consciousness like a crank on a record player.

You're embedding truth deep into the subconscious, until it replaces the fear, the panic, the blockage.

Soon enough, you'll feel it — the shift.

Your vision clears. Your body relaxes. Your thoughts stabilize.

And then, inevitably, the manifestation follows.

It may be health. It may be money. It may be peace.

But it will come.

One student once asked me:

"Why does everything seem to fall apart right before a big break-through?"

Because you're clearing out the garbage.

The subconscious — loaded with fear and generational programming — starts to purge.

It's the "darkness before the dawn."

These old derelicts rise up to be burned off. You don't resist them. You don't feed them.

You keep repeating:

"I cast this burden on the Christ within, and I go free."

And then... you are.

When you're surrounded by pressure — disease, debt, rejection, the unknown — the average person collapses. But the one who understands spiritual law does something completely different.

He claps his cymbals and gives thanks.

Like Jehoshaphat in the Bible, he celebrates before the victory.

He gives thanks before the change.

He stands in the darkness and says, "I already won."

That's what casting the burden leads to: clear vision in the dark.

A student once asked, "How long do I have to stay in the dark?"

I told her:

"Until you can see in the dark."

Faith without action is worthless.

"Faith without works is dead."

You don't get results just by knowing the truth — you have to move like it's real.

Jesus understood this. Before He multiplied the loaves and fishes, He told everyone to sit down — as if the food was already there.

That's active faith.

It's the bridge between belief and reality.

Here's an example that hits hard:

A woman was separated from her husband — the man she loved. He cut all contact. Refused reconciliation. Nothing worked.

But she learned the law.

She denied the separation.

She declared:

"There is no separation in Divine Mind. I cannot be separated from the love and companionship that are mine by divine right."

And then she did something radical:

She set a place for him at the table. Every day.

That was her act of faith.

That was her message to the subconscious: He's coming back.

A year passed. No movement.

And then one day — he walked back into her life.

That's how it works.

Not always fast. But always precise.

The subconscious isn't just moved by logic — it's moved by rhythm, music, motion, and symbolic action.

One student used her Victrola (record player) to get into a flow state.

Music snapped her into alignment — and suddenly, her imagination became a weapon again.

Another woman danced while making affirmations — and her words carried massive charge because the body and rhythm helped burn them into her system.

Don't just think truth.

Move with it. Breathe it. Live it.

The subconscious responds to full-body belief.

And remember: never despise the day of small things.

Right before a breakthrough, you'll get signs of land. Just like Columbus spotting birds and seaweed before seeing America.

Don't mistake the preview for the prize.

One woman declared a full set of dishes.

Not long after, a friend gave her a single cracked plate.

She said, "Well... this isn't what I asked for."

I told her:

"That's your sign of land. It means the real thing is close. Treat it like evidence."

And sure enough — the full set came.

Here's the secret most people miss:

Make-believe works.

If you "make believe" you're wealthy, loved, successful — and you persist — you'll pull it into reality.

Why?

Because the subconscious can't tell the difference between imagination and fact. It just takes orders.

Children do this instinctively. They play rich, happy, invincible. That's why Christ said:

"Unless you become as little children, you can't enter the Kingdom."

The Kingdom isn't a place.

It's a state of being where manifestation is normal — and resistance doesn't exist.

There was a woman I knew — broke by every measure. But she never let it touch her.

Her rich friends kept warning her: "Be careful. Save your money."

She ignored them.

She spent her earnings on hats and gifts. Laughed. Felt good. Dreamed about "rings and things." But with no envy. Just pure expectancy.

Eventually, she married into wealth.

She didn't chase it. She became it.

The money showed up because she refused to feel poor.

But if you want to live like this, you have to deal with fear.

Fear is misdirected energy. It has to be rerouted — converted into faith.

Jesus asked:

"Why are you afraid, oh you of little faith?"

Because fear and faith can't occupy the same space.

You want to destroy fear?

Walk into it.

Every time someone asks me, "How do I get rid of fear?"

I say:

"Walk toward what you're afraid of."

Not away. Not around. Straight through.
"The lion takes its fierceness from your fear."
Walk up to the lion, and it vanishes.
Run, and it chases you.

So when the fear shows up — and it will — don't resist.
Don't collapse.
Don't numb out.
Face it. Speak the truth. Act in faith.
Clap your cymbals in the dark.
And walk into the thing you're sure will eat you alive.
That's where the power is.
That's where everything turns.
I've shown you how the lion disappears when you stop running from it.
The same law applies to money.
Lack only exists when you fear letting go.
When you grip. When you hoard. When you try to "save" your way into wealth.
Many of my students have broken out of poverty by doing one thing: spending fearlessly.
They stopped treating money like it was scarce, fragile, or something they had to beg for. They stopped thinking of it as separate from themselves.
They realized the truth:
God is both the Giver and the Gift.
And if you are aligned with the Giver, then you are inseparable from the Gift.
One of the strongest affirmations you can say:
"I now thank God the Giver for God the Gift."
Say it like it's done. Because it is.

But sometimes the poverty program runs so deep, it takes a crisis — a shock — to blow it out of the subconscious.

Fear is stubborn. And most people won't let it go until they're forced.
So when something big happens — a financial collapse, a health scare, a confrontation — don't curse it.
That's your spiritual dynamite.
It's blasting out the old structure. Making space for something real to be built.

Start watching yourself like a hawk.
Is this decision coming from fear — or faith?
• Do you say yes to people out of fear of being disliked?
• Do you avoid a job, a city, a relationship out of fear of failure?
• Do you not invest, not spend, not give — because you don't trust the return?
That's fear. And fear always costs more than faith.
Every hour, ask yourself: Am I serving fear or faith?
"Choose ye this day whom ye shall serve."
Make a choice. Then back it with action.

Maybe your fear is tied to a person.
Someone who intimidates, triggers, or controls you.
Then face them.
Stop avoiding. Walk right into the conversation.
They will either reveal themselves as a golden link in the chain of your good, or they'll disappear without conflict.
But the fear? It dies the second you stop giving it power.

Maybe your fear is disease. Germs. Death.
Then walk into the space where fear tells you not to go — and do it calmly.
You only contract what you're vibrating with.
Fear drops your frequency to the level of the problem.
Faith raises your frequency above it.
You cannot catch what you're not aligned with.

Germs are not real in Divine Mind.

They're projections from the carnal mind — fear objectified.

In the superconscious, they don't exist.

In truth, nothing rooted in fear can exist in the presence of spiritual certainty.

Your release — your transformation — can happen in an instant.

"In the twinkling of an eye," everything can shift.

The second you realize that evil has no power, that fear is false authority,

that lack is an illusion — the world you see dissolves.

The old matrix falls away.

And what takes its place?

The fourth-dimensional world.

The World of the Wondrous.

The place where time collapses, and things move as fast as you believe.

It's already there. Waiting.

But you can't drag fear with you.

You can't bring your backup plans, your doubts, or your guilt.

You walk into it clean. Free.

"And I saw a new heaven, and a new earth...

and there shall be no more death, nor sorrow, nor crying, nor pain.

For the former things are passed away."

That's not a myth. That's a spiritual destination.

And it begins the moment you choose faith.

Chapter Seven

Real Love Doesn't Chase — It Attracts
Everyone on this planet is going through one universal test:
Love.
Not the Hallmark version. Not emotional need. Not guilt-drenched obligation.
Real love.
The kind that's selfless. The kind that gives without clinging.
The kind that radiates power without needing permission.
"A new commandment I give unto you: that ye love one another."
Ouspensky called love a cosmic force — the key that unlocks the fourth dimension, the World of the Wondrous.
And yet most people don't even recognize love when it's in front of them. They confuse it with fear, control, jealousy, and insecurity.
But real love isn't fragile.
Real love doesn't need to be returned to be valid.
It stands on its own. It magnetizes. It draws.
It doesn't chase — it attracts.

A woman came to me once in full breakdown.
She was in love with a man who had left her, chased other women, and told her he would never marry her.
She was enraged.
Jealous. Bitter.
Wishing him pain because of how much she "loved" him.

I told her straight:

"That's not love. That's hatred with a romantic costume."

She said, "But how could he leave me when I loved him so much?"

I answered:

"You're not loving him — you're hating him for not loving you.

You can never receive what you've never given.

Start giving real love — selfless, unconditional, clean.

Bless him. Wherever he is. And stop demanding anything in return."

She hesitated. "I'm not blessing him unless I know where he is."

Exactly. That's the proof she wasn't ready yet.

I told her this:

"When you send out real love, it has to come back.

Either from this man or his divine equivalent.

And if he's not your divine selection, trust me — you won't want him."

She kept working on herself. Slowly, the bitterness faded.

I taught her something from an Indian brotherhood:

They greet each other not with "hello," but with:

"I salute the Divinity in you."

They say it to people. They say it to wild animals.

And they're never harmed — because they only see God in others.

I told her to do the same. To look at this man and say:

"I see your Divine Self only. I see you as God sees you — perfect, made in His image."

Eventually, something clicked. One day she said it sincerely:

"God bless the Cap, wherever he is."

That's when I knew she had arrived. She had become a complete circle.

No more chasing. No more reacting.

Within weeks — they were married.

When I asked what changed, she said:

"A miracle. I woke up one day, and all the pain was gone. That night I saw him. He asked me to marry him. We were married within a week. He's completely devoted now."

That's how spiritual law works.

You change. The world follows.

"No man is your enemy. No man is your friend. Every man is your teacher."

Everyone who enters your life is showing you what you still need to master.

That woman's lesson was selfless love.

It's a required course for everyone — and most people fail the first few times.

Now let's talk about loss.

Most suffering comes from violating the law — saying one thing, feeling another, living in contradiction.

I knew a woman with a great husband.

But she kept saying, "I don't care about marriage. It's not for me."

She didn't appreciate what she had.

She barely noticed him unless he was in front of her.

Eventually, he left — for someone who valued him.

She came to me, shocked and resentful.

I said:

"You got exactly what you spoke into being.

You said you didn't care about being married —

and now, you're not."

She got it. Fast.

"People get what they want — and then feel hurt by the result."

She accepted it. Realized they were both happier apart. And moved on in peace.

Another example:

A man came to me — flatlined in life. Depressed. Broke.

His wife had been dabbling in numerology and told him, "You'll never amount to anything. You're a two."

I said:

"I don't care if your number is two, twelve, or 666.

You're a perfect idea in Divine Mind.

And we're going to call forth the success already designed for you by Infinite Intelligence."

That man went on to turn everything around.

Because the numbers didn't define him.

Her beliefs didn't define him.

His alignment with Divine Mind did.

Real love begins when you stop needing and start seeing.

Seeing the good.

Seeing the divine pattern.

Seeing the truth behind the chaos.

When you stop controlling and start trusting.

When you stop fearing and start blessing.

When you stop clinging and start radiating.

And when you can say, from a place of peace:

"God bless them, wherever they are."

That's when the miracle shows up.

Or something better does.

You don't succeed at anything unless you love it.

That's the rule.

The man who finds success in business? He enjoys the work.

The artist who creates his masterpiece? He paints from passion — not a paycheck.

The "potboiler" art — made to survive — is always something to live down.

And when it comes to money, here's what you need to know:

You will never attract what you secretly despise.

Plenty of people stay broke because they hold contempt for money and the people who have it.

They say, "Money means nothing to me."
Or worse, "I can't stand rich people."
And then they wonder why their bank accounts are empty.
Artists are notorious for this. One even said to me, about a peer:
"He's no good — he actually has money in the bank."
That kind of thinking repels supply. Period.
To attract anything, you must be in harmony with it.

Money is not evil.
Money is freedom. Money is choice. Money is God in motion — when used correctly.
It must circulate. It must be used.
If you hoard it out of fear, you'll lose it — and you'll lose other things along with it.
You're not being told to live broke. You're not told to avoid assets.
"The barns of the righteous shall be full."
Have stocks. Have land. Own it all.
But when life asks you to let money go, let it go — cheerfully, confidently.
Because letting go makes space for more.
That's how the universal bank works.
And the Great Bank of the Infinite never defaults.

You want to see what hoarding does?
Watch the movie Greed.
A woman wins $5,000 in a lottery.
But she won't spend it.
She lets her husband suffer and starve.
Eventually, she scrubs floors for a living — still guarding her precious stash.
In the end? She's murdered.
The money's taken. The obsession kills her.
This is where "the love of money is the root of all evil."

Not because money is bad — but because she made it her god.
Money isn't meant to be clutched.
It's meant to be channeled.

I knew a woman with extreme wealth.
But she hoarded every penny. Rarely gave. Constantly bought for herself — things she didn't use.
She had sixty-seven necklaces — all stored in tissue paper, unworn.
Her closets? Full of unworn clothes. Her vaults? Full of locked-away jewelry.
You want to know what happened?
Her arms began to paralyze.
She literally couldn't let go.
Eventually, she was declared incompetent. Her fortune — handed over to others.
Spiritual law handled what she refused to handle herself.
Use it — or lose it.

You violate the law of love, and you pay for it — every time.
- Criticism becomes sickness.
- Jealousy becomes destruction.
- Resentment becomes disease.

Love isn't optional. It's law.
Without love, you become:
"Sounding brass and tinkling cymbals."
Noise. Empty. Off-key.

I had a student who came to me month after month to clear resentment.
She kept making progress — but one woman still had her trapped.
"I've forgiven everyone," she said, "except her."
But that one woman kept her energy poisoned.
She stuck with the work. Bit by bit, she chipped away the grudge.
Then one day — she came in glowing.

"She said something to me," she told me,
"and instead of reacting, I was kind.
I felt no rage. I felt love. And she apologized!
It was like magic."
But it wasn't magic.
It was law.
Resentment is a prison.
Forgiveness is release.
When you clear the static, your frequency rises.
And with that elevation comes clarity, power — and peace.

Love works in business too.
Love works especially in business.
A woman once came to me, frustrated about her employer.
Cold. Critical. Clearly didn't want her there.
(We'll get to that outcome in the next section.)
But remember this:
The law of love isn't just about relationships —
it's about alignment in every field.
Love clears the channel.
Love opens the gates.
And when you're truly in that state — giving freely, holding nothing —
everything changes.
Including your money.
Including your enemies.
Including you.
One of my students once told me she couldn't love her boss.
"She's a marble woman," she said—cold, stone-faced, impossible.
I told her, "Salute the Divinity in her. Send her love anyway."
She rolled her eyes.
So I told her the story of the sculptor who picked out an ugly slab of
marble. When asked why, he said:
"Because there's an angel in the marble."

And he carved it.

That shut her up. She agreed to try.

A week later, she came back lit up.

"I did what you told me. She's been kind to me all week—and she even took me for a ride in her car."

That's what happens when you stop reacting to the surface—and start seeing what's underneath.

People are haunted by guilt over things they did years ago.

And if the wrong can't be fixed directly, the energy of it can still be neutralized.

How?

Do something kind now. Balance it. Clean the slate.

Dwelling in regret doesn't fix anything.

It corrodes your health. It pollutes your energy. It keeps you in the past, locked in shame.

"This one thing I do: forgetting those things which are behind, and reaching forth to the things which are before."

Let it go—or it'll pull you down.

I had a woman once ask me to treat her for happiness.

Why?

"Because my sorrow is making me so irritable, I keep hurting my family and racking up more karma."

At least she was honest.

I treated another woman mourning the death of her daughter.

I denied all belief in loss, grief, and separation, and affirmed:

"God is her joy, her peace, her love."

She gained her poise instantly. Peace flooded in.

But the next day, her son brought a message: "Please stop the treatment."

Why?

"She's so happy, it doesn't feel respectable."

That's what happens when mortal mind clings to its grief. It enjoys the sorrow. It builds an identity out of it.

Some people brag about their problems.
They wear pain like a badge.
They think suffering gives them significance.
And so they always have something new to complain about—because they're creating it, over and over again.
Same with worry.
For years, people thought a woman who didn't worry about her kids was a bad mother.
Now we know the truth:
Mother-fear creates most of the disasters it tries to prevent.
Fear builds vivid pictures of sickness and accidents—and the subconscious treats those images like instructions.
It doesn't filter. It executes.

Real power is when a mother can say:
"I place my child in God's hands. He is divinely protected."
And believe it.
I knew one woman who woke in the middle of the night, sensing danger around her brother.
Instead of spiraling into fear, she declared:
"Man is a perfect idea in Divine Mind.
He is always in his right place and divinely protected."
The next day, she found out her brother had been near an explosion in a mine—but had come out untouched.

You are your brother's keeper.
Not through control.
Through thought.
Every person you love lives in your consciousness. And if your consciousness is full of fear, they're vulnerable. But if it's full of faith?

"They that dwell in the secret place of the Most High shall abide under the shadow of the Almighty."

"No evil shall befall thee. No plague shall come near thy dwelling."

This isn't poetry.

This is policy—spiritual law in action.

"Perfect love casts out fear."

"He who fears has not been made perfect in love."

"Love is the fulfilling of the Law."

Not revenge.

Not control.

Not guilt or sacrifice.

Love.

When you walk in real love, not emotionalism—not manipulation—but clear, steady, nonreactive divine love... you become untouchable.

And you make everyone around you safer.

Chapter Eight

Intuition—Ask, Then Move
"In all thy ways acknowledge Him, and He shall direct thy paths."
Nothing is out of reach for the person who knows two things:

1. The power of their word.
2. How to follow the lead when it shows up.

Your word moves unseen forces. It builds your body. It rebuilds your world. So what you say matters—and what you do next matters even more.

Once you've spoken your desire into motion, you don't run around trying to force results.

You wait for the lead.

I've been asked hundreds of times: "How do I make something happen? How do I get the result?"

The answer is simple:

Speak the word. Then shut up and listen.

You say:

"Infinite Spirit, show me the way.

Let me know if there's anything I need to do.

Give me a clear lead."

That lead might come as:

- A hunch.
- A line in a book.
- A comment from a stranger.

- A smell, a sound, a strange pull in your gut.

The only wrong move is ignoring it.

Here's what it looks like in practice:

A woman needed a large sum of money.

She declared:

"Infinite Spirit, open the way for my immediate supply.

Let all that is mine by divine right now reach me, in great avalanches of abundance.

Give me a clear lead."

The next thought she had?

"Give $100 to a friend who's helped you."

She told the friend, who said: "Wait for a second lead."

So she did.

That same day, another woman said, casually:

"I gave someone a dollar today. It was as big for me as a hundred would be for you."

Clear. Direct. Confirmed.

She gave the hundred—and shortly after, a large financial windfall came her way.

Why?

Because giving triggers receiving.

If you want to move money, move money.

Tithing—giving one-tenth—is an ancient law, and it works. Not because of superstition, but because it sets your consciousness to circulate.

You become a conduit, not a dam.

But it only works if it's done cheerfully.

God loves a cheerful giver.

Pay bills cheerfully. Tip generously. Send money out with a blessing, not a death grip.

This makes you master over money—not its slave.

Here's the trap most people fall into:
They get the vision, but they don't take the action.
They say, "I can feel abundance!"
And then they walk away from the opportunity to buy the coat, book the ticket, or make the offer.
They choke. They shrink. They kill the charge.
Vision without action is just fantasy.
You saw what happened with the man and the fur-lined coat. He bought it on a hunch—spent nearly all he had—and within a month closed a deal worth ten thousand.
That coat aligned him with the result.

Same principle applies with work.
A woman came to me asking for a job.
I didn't just say, "Let's get her a position."
I said:
"Let's get her the right position.
The one that already exists in Divine Mind.
The one that brings satisfaction and success."
Soon, she had three offers—two in New York, one in Palm Beach.
She couldn't decide.
So I said:
"Ask for the lead."
Time was running out. Then one morning she called and said:
"I woke up and could smell Palm Beach."
That was the lead.
She accepted the job. It turned out to be a total win.

The best leads come when you're not thinking about it.
I was walking down the street one day, minding my own business, when I got a sudden pull to go to a bakery two blocks away.
My logic said, "You don't want anything from there."
But I've learned: don't argue with guidance.

So I went.

(We'll cover what happened next in the continuation.)

Here's the takeaway:

Ask. Wait. Move when the lead hits.

You don't get points for overthinking.

You don't get results by forcing it.

You get results by aligning your word with your faith, and then following through when the next step shows up—no matter how weird, random, or impractical it looks at the time.

Trust the pattern.

Then walk it.

Intuition doesn't owe you a reason.

It doesn't explain.

It doesn't rationalize.

It just points the way—and it's up to you to follow it.

One day I had a sudden urge to visit a bakery two blocks out of my way.

There was nothing I wanted. My logic said, "Skip it."

But I've learned: never argue with the nudge.

So I went. And on the way out, I ran into a woman I'd been thinking of—a woman in serious need of the kind of help I was equipped to give. So often, you're guided toward one thing but the real reason is something else entirely.

Intuition is a spiritual faculty. It doesn't operate on logic or linear steps.

It's the voice of Divine Mind cutting through noise.

You might even receive the lead while in treatment.

It may seem irrelevant.

But nothing real is random—especially when you're aligned.

I once gave a treatment to a class, asking that everyone receive a clear lead.

Afterward, a woman came up and said:

"I suddenly got the urge to take my furniture out of storage and get my

own apartment."
She had come for a health issue.
I told her, "Perfect. That's not random. Your congestion isn't just phys-ical—it's spiritual. You've been hoarding things, and it's showing up in your body. Get the stuff moving, and your health will follow."
That's the law of use.
Let things sit idle, and you create stagnation—first in your life, then in your cells.

You can have a miraculous healing by aligning with the truth:
"My body is a perfect idea in Divine Mind. Whole. Complete. Func-tional."
But if you go right back to resentment, guilt, fear, or hoarding?
The sickness returns.
Why?
Because your soul—the subconscious—is still running the old tape.
Jesus knew this. That's why He said:
"Go and sin no more, lest a worse thing come upon you."
Healing isn't just a reset. It's a reprogramming.

Let's talk condemnation.
Every time you judge someone, criticize them, or resent them—you in-vite that same energy into your own life.
I had a woman whose husband had left her for someone else. She couldn't stop condemning the other woman.
"She knew he was married. She had no right."
I said:
"Bless her and move on. If you don't, you'll attract the same situation."
She refused. A year later, she got involved with a married man herself.
You touch the live wire of judgment—and you get shocked.

Then there's the problem of indecision.
It paralyzes people. Wrecks momentum. Kills opportunity.

You want to break it?

Start affirming:

"I am always under direct inspiration. I make right decisions quickly and clearly."

Do this until it reprograms your subconscious.

Soon, you'll move with clarity instead of hesitation.

One big warning here:

Stay off the psychic plane.

It's full of noise—random minds, conflicting energies, and emotional static.

It's not the voice of God. It's the echo chamber of man.

When you open your mind to "whatever comes," you invite anything in.

Even horoscopes and numerology can trap you on the karmic loop.

They tell you what was, not what's divinely possible.

I know a man who, according to his chart, should've been dead years ago.

He's alive.

He's thriving.

He's leading one of the most powerful spiritual movements in the country.

Why?

Because he refused to bow to a bad prediction.

If you've ever received a negative prophecy, cancel it now:

"Every false prophecy is dissolved.

Every plan not authored by the Divine is wiped clean.

The perfect will of God is now done."

But if you were ever told something good—something about love, success, or joy—hold it close.

Expect it.

Prepare for it.

And it will arrive—by the law of expectancy.

Your personal will isn't meant to bulldoze life into submission.
It's meant to back the universal will.
"I will that the will of God be done."
Use your willpower to hold the perfect vision.
Not to control outcomes.
Not to obsess.
Hold it steady—and trust the pattern.
The prodigal son's power wasn't just in his return—it was in his decision.
"I will arise and go to my Father."
Make that same choice.
And watch everything shift.
Leaving behind the "husks and swine" of mortal thinking—resentment, fear, lack—isn't easy.
It takes will to choose faith over fear.
For most people, fear is the reflex. Faith is the stretch.
But once you wake up spiritually, you start to see it for what it is:
Every external problem?
Just a mirror of internal disorder.
You trip on the sidewalk? You're stumbling in consciousness.
You get blindsided by people? You were throwing mental punches at someone else.

One of my students proved this.
She was walking down the street, full of judgment, condemning another woman in her head:
"That woman is the most disagreeable woman on earth."
In that moment, three Boy Scouts came flying around a corner and nearly mowed her down.
She didn't blame the kids. She knew what she'd done.
She stopped and immediately corrected her energy:

Called on the law of forgiveness.
Saluted the divinity in the woman she had condemned.
Cause and effect. Thought and consequence.
Wisdom doesn't come from experience.
It comes from recognizing the pattern.
"Wisdom's ways are pleasantness, and all her paths are peace."

When you've placed a demand on the Universal Bank—when you've spoken the word—expect to be surprised.
Sometimes, everything seems to go wrong.
That's how you know it's working.

Take this example:
A woman had loaned $2,000 to a relative who later died without repaying her or mentioning it in her will. No written agreement. No proof.
Just loss.
And a lot of anger.
Years went by. Still no repayment.
Then she learned: there's no loss in Divine Mind. Ever.
So she got to work—first by dropping the resentment.
Because resentment locks the vault.
She declared:
"I deny loss.
There is no loss in Divine Mind.
What's mine by divine right must return—either directly or by equivalent."
Then the chain reaction began.

Her landlord raised the rent. Unjust? Maybe.
But she didn't flinch.
She said:
"If the rent's going up, then I'm getting richer.
God is my supply."

What the landlord didn't realize is he'd forgotten to reinsert a critical clause in the new lease:

If the building sold, tenants couldn't be forced out for 90 days.

Divine mistake.

Soon, he got an offer to sell the building. The tenants were legally locked in.

So he started paying them to leave.

First, $200 offers.

Then, a few months later—he came to her with an offer:

"Will you give up your lease for $1,500?"

She got the nudge: this is it.

But she remembered her earlier agreement with other tenants—they'd act together.

She asked them.

They said:

"If they're offering $1,500, they'll give you $2,000."

They were right.

She got the check.

$2,000—restored.

That's how the law works.

There was no "coincidence." No luck. No karma.

It was a spiritual invoice finally being paid—once she stopped blocking the flow.

The injustice?

It was just the setup.

"I will restore to you the years the locusts have eaten."

And what are the locusts?

- Doubt
- Fear
- Regret
- Resentment

They devour your time, energy, health, and opportunities.
But it was never the world robbing you.
You give or withhold from yourself. No one else does it.

You're here to prove God.
Not just preach or philosophize—but prove it.
How?
Bring abundance where there was lack.
Bring justice where there was betrayal.
Bring peace where there was chaos.
Until you do that, your faith is still theory.

"Prove me now, saith the Lord,
if I will not open the windows of heaven,
and pour out a blessing so large,
you won't have room to receive it."
There's nothing noble about settling.
There's nothing spiritual about staying small.
The Bank of the Infinite is stocked and open.
Your only job?
Stop slamming the door shut with your own thoughts.

Chapter Nine

P erfect Self-Expression – Unlock the Plan
    "No wind can drive my bark astray, nor change the tide of destiny."
There is something only you are meant to do.
A role only you can fill.
A lane no one else can drive.
That's not feel-good talk. That's reality.
You have a Divine Design—and you're either aligned with it, or you're flailing around in someone else's pattern.

It doesn't matter if you know what that design is right now.
Most people don't.
But the demand is the first step:
"Infinite Spirit, reveal the Divine Design for my life.
Release the genius within me.
Let me see the perfect plan clearly."
Once you say that, don't expect things to stay the same.
The truth is, most people are way off path—working jobs that kill them, living lives that shrink them, or chasing status instead of purpose.
When the Divine Design starts coming in, it might feel like a storm at first. But it's clearing the garbage so the real can land.

Here's the rule:
The perfect plan includes the full square of life:

- Health
- Wealth
- Love
- Self-expression

If something's missing, you're not in full alignment yet.

But you can be.

A man came to me with only seven cents to his name. He gave me one—bold move—and said:

"Speak the word for my perfect self-expression and prosperity."

I did.

A year later, he showed up with money, health, purpose, and a huge smile.

He said:

"Right after you spoke the word, I got an offer in another city. My whole life turned around."

The shift wasn't the job. It was the alignment.

Self-expression doesn't always mean the spotlight.

Some women are built to be world-class mothers, wives, and homemakers.

That is divine work—if it's your work.

There's no one-size-fits-all destiny.

There's only your destiny.

And when it shows up, it won't feel like "work."

It'll feel like you've finally taken the weight vest off.

You're not here to force a vision. You're here to catch it.

Don't waste time forcing mental pictures of what you think your future should look like.

Instead, ask for the Divine Design to land—and watch for flashes, dreams, spontaneous knowing, a sudden image of what you're supposed to build.

That's the one you hold.

That's your lane.

"The thing man seeks is seeking him.

The telephone was seeking Bell."

And parents:

Stop projecting your baggage onto your kids.

Don't script out their future like a legacy project. Speak for their own design:

"Let the God in this child have perfect expression.

Let the Divine Design of their mind, body, and purpose manifest through life and eternity."

It's their life, not yours.

Fear is the usual enemy of self-expression.

- Fear of failure.
- Fear of rejection.
- Fear of being seen.

But fear is just energy turned backward. Flip it.

Speak:

"Infinite Intelligence speaks through me.

I am fearless, clear, and guided."

Stage fright? Gone.

Writer's block? Cracked open.

That "I'm not enough" feeling? Overwritten.

A young boy once asked me to help him pass his school exams. I told him:

"Say: I am one with Infinite Intelligence. I know everything I need to know."

He passed math with flying colors.

But for history? He thought he didn't need help.

He failed that part.

The point?
Never get cocky. Never go solo.
When you stop leaning on Divine Mind, the cracks show fast.

One woman traveled through multiple countries where she didn't know the language.
She relied on divine guidance for everything—transportation, luggage, rooms—and everything went smoothly.
When she got home, where she knew the language, she stopped asking for guidance.
She figured she had it under control.
That's when everything started going sideways.

You're not here to manage life manually.
You're here to sync with the pattern.
When you move in that rhythm, doors fly open, resistance drops, and what's meant for you finds you.
Don't bury your gift.
"To whom much is given, much is required."
There's a cost to playing small.

Don't be the "wicked and slothful servant" who buried his talent.
The penalty for wasted potential isn't just lost opportunity—it's spiritual debt.
You came here to express something divine.
You came here to build, create, love, serve, or lead in a way no one else can.
Don't die full.
Die empty.
Everything went sideways. Her bags were delayed. Her travel plans imploded in confusion and static.
Why? She had dropped the thread. She forgot to "practice the presence."

She stopped checking in with the source.

"In all thy ways acknowledge Him"—that means all. Not just when the chips are down or the skies are blue.

Because sometimes, what seems small isn't.

Fulton stared at boiling water and saw a steamship.

One of the most common blocks I've seen?

Resistance and control.

People want miracles but give God instructions.

They fixate on how it has to happen, who it has to come through, and when it needs to land.

And when it doesn't go their way, they panic or give up.

That's not faith. That's dictatorship.

The law doesn't follow your terms.

It follows alignment.

You must be an open circuit—nonresistant, available, and aligned.

"My way, not your way," says the Infinite.

Your job? Get out of the way.

Poise is power.

That's the real endgame of all this:

A state where you are so aligned, nothing throws you off-center.

"Be still and know."

Be still—not frantic.

Be still—not begging.

Be still—and command from presence.

That's how the $2,000 showed up.

That's how the man came back.

That's how the deals, jobs, homes, and healing land.

Anger? Kills your power.

Fear? Same.

Worry? Just faith inverted and aimed at the wrong target.

"Whatever is not of faith is sin."
Not sin in the old-school, fire-and-brimstone sense—
But sin in that it separates you from your source, from your flow, from the Divine Circuit.
And separation leads to sickness, failure, confusion, and collapse.

Want to clear fear?
Walk up to the thing you're afraid of.
That's the whole game.
A woman once had to deliver a tough message to a friend.
Every part of her ego said, "Don't do it. Don't get involved."
But she had promised. So she walked into the lion's den—head-on, no flinching.
And what happened?
Before she could even speak, her friend said, "Oh, that doesn't matter—she's out of town."
The thing vanished the moment she faced it.

The finish line? It's already there.
But most people never cross it—because they stop running three feet before the tape.
They believe in incompletion. They carry a subconscious story of "I always get close, but never quite make it."
Break that.
Say this:
"In Divine Mind, there is only completion.
My demonstration is finished. My work is finished. My supply is finished.
I give thanks it is already done—under grace, in a perfect way."
Then prepare. Act like it's landed. Finish something.

A student once came to me, needing money.
I asked, "Do you leave things unfinished?"

She said yes. It was her habit to start projects and abandon them halfway.

So I told her: "Go home and finish something. Anything."

She picked up an old sewing project and completed it with care.

Shortly after, money came—in the strangest way.

Her husband was accidentally paid twice.

He told the company.

Their reply?

"Keep it."

The law is no joke.

It doesn't miss.

But you can block it with your unfinished thoughts, your resistance, or your refusal to release the how.

Stay in poise. Practice presence. Finish what you start. Walk toward fear. Speak with faith.

The Divine Design is already yours.

But you must align to collect it.

When you ask—and you believe—you receive. That's it.

God makes the channel. Your job is to open it.

And when it comes to choosing between talents, don't get caught in indecision or false humility. Ask to be shown.

"Show me my lane. Show me what gift you want me to use. Make it clear. Make it bold."

Then act. Don't hesitate.

When it drops, it'll come ready to go. I've seen people walk into entire new lives with zero prep and thrive—because it was theirs by divine design.

So say it:

"I am fully equipped for the Divine Plan of my life."

And mean it.

A lot of people like to give, but they choke on receiving. Pride. Shame.

Guilt.

They block the very thing they've been praying for.

Don't do that.

God repays. The universe circulates. You don't get to control how it comes back—just know that it will.

I've seen people give away thousands joyfully, then reject a gift when it came. That rejection closed their channel. And what happened? Their money got jammed up. They went into debt for the exact amount they had refused.

Never refuse your return.

All gifts come from God. The person giving? Just the delivery guy.

Accept the stamp. Accept the compliment. Accept the cash. Say thank you.

You're not being greedy—you're staying in flow.

"The Lord loveth a cheerful giver"—sure.

But He also loves a cheerful receiver.

You want to know why some people are born rich and others broke? Healthy vs. sick? Free vs. trapped?

It's not chance. It's not luck. There's always a cause.

It's memory in the soul. Carried over. That's Karma.

You don't remember the game you played last time, but your subconscious does.

The rich man programmed abundance. The sick man imprinted failure. And both are still living out those stories—until one of them wakes up and says:

"No more."

That's what you're here for.

To break the cycle.

To finish the lesson.

To align with your true design and move past the old scripts.

You don't have to keep coming back. You don't have to keep reliving the fall.

Birth and death are man's ideas. They're not real. The real man was never born, and never dies.

"As he was in the beginning, is now, and ever shall be."

Your freedom isn't about running away from life. It's about fulfilling it.

Executing the plan you came here to complete.

When you do, the doors open.

The fear dies.

The karma clears.

And the Divine says:

"Well done, good and faithful servant. You finished what you came here to finish.

You ruled your mind. You ruled your fear.

Now—step into joy. Step into life."

That's how you win.

Epilogue

AFFIRMATIONS AND REALITY
"Thou shalt also decree a thing, and it shall be established unto thee."

That's not poetry. That's power.

Everything good you want is already built and waiting in the invisible—the blueprint is done. It's not about making it happen; it's about declaring it and opening the gate. The tool? Your words. The trap? Using them carelessly.

Idle talk of failure, misfortune, or doubt is how most people curse themselves daily. They don't even realize they're making decrees.

That's why your declarations must be precise.

Want a new house? A real partner? A next-level job?

Don't ask randomly—ask correctly.

"Infinite Spirit, open the way for my right home, my right friend, my right position. I give thanks it now manifests, under grace, in a perfect way."

That last part matters. Under grace. In a perfect way.

One woman demanded a thousand dollars. She got it—after her daughter was injured and they got a settlement. The money came, but not the way she wanted.

So what she should have said was:

"I give thanks the $1,000 that is mine by divine right is now released and reaches me under grace, in a perfect way."

This is grown-up spiritual law. No loopholes. No sloppy wording. You'll get what you declare. So declare wisely.

You'll never receive beyond what your subconscious thinks is possible. You want to expand your life? Expand your belief. Expect bigger. Stretch your ceiling.

One student asked for exactly $600. He got it.

Later, he found out $1,000 was on the table—but he only got what he asked for.

"They limited the Holy One of Israel."

Don't limit the law. Start saying:

"I give thanks the enormous sums of money that are mine by divine right are now released and reach me, under grace, in perfect ways."

Because money isn't just numbers. It's consciousness.

The French have a story: a poor man receives a gold nugget and is told it'll make him rich forever. He believes it—and he becomes rich.

Years later, he gives the nugget to another poor man, who gets it tested—it's brass. Worthless.

The first man didn't need the gold. He needed the belief.

So do you.

Real faith doesn't beg. It acts. It moves. It thanks in advance.

"Before you call, I will answer."

So you speak as if it's already done. You thank like it's already here. You behave like the cheque is already in the mail.

A woman once needed a large sum fast. She asked for a sign—a lead. While walking through a store, she saw a beautiful pink letter opener. She felt drawn to it.

Then the thought hit: "I don't have a letter opener worthy of a cheque that size."

She bought it.

That wasn't just shopping. That was activating faith.

A few weeks later, she received the money.

The pink papercutter was her bridge between belief and manifestation.

Prayer is not groveling. It's command, demand, praise, and thanks.
"Give us this day our daily bread."
"Forgive us our debts."
"Thine is the kingdom."
You don't ask like a beggar—you speak like a partner in divine creation.
You're not hoping. You're activating. You're aligning. And when it's time to move, you move.
But when it's time to stand still—you stand still. That's discipline. That's trust.

Final reminder:
What you decree, you create.
What you believe, you receive.
What you fear, you attract.
What you affirm, you become.
Your job isn't to "figure it out."
Your job is to speak it, believe it, and align like it's already done.
And it will be.
A man once spent the night in an old farmhouse. The windows in his room had been nailed shut, and in the middle of the night, he woke up feeling like he couldn't breathe. In the dark, he stumbled toward what he thought was the window, desperate for air. He smashed the glass with his fist, took in deep gulps of what he believed was fresh air, and slept peacefully.
The next morning, he discovered he had actually broken the glass of a bookcase—not the window. The windows had remained sealed all night. What refreshed him was the belief that he was breathing clean air. His thought alone had supplied what his body needed.
This story is a powerful reminder of the mind's influence. Once you begin a manifestation—what we used to call "demonstration"—you must not turn back. "Let not the one who wavers think they will receive any-

thing from the Lord." In other words, don't second-guess. Don't compromise. Commit fully to your vision.

As one student put it, "When I ask God for something, I put my foot down and say, 'Father, I won't settle for anything less than what I asked for—only more!'" That's the mindset.

There's often a delay right before your breakthrough. Why? Because it's only when you truly let go—stop trying to control every outcome—that Infinite Intelligence can do its work. Miracles tend to show up at the eleventh hour, just after we've exhausted our need to interfere.

For example, a woman once came to me frustrated because she kept losing or breaking her glasses. We traced it back to something she kept saying: "I wish I could just get rid of these glasses!" The subconscious doesn't filter sarcasm or frustration—it takes everything literally. She didn't actually affirm improved vision; she affirmed a desire to be without glasses. So, they kept disappearing or breaking.

Two major mindsets cause loss: one is depreciation—not appreciating what you have. The other is fear—constantly imagining something being taken away. Both of these mental habits create loss.

Another example: A woman was walking on a windy, stormy day. Her umbrella blew inside-out, and she dreaded making a first impression on new people while holding a broken umbrella. She couldn't just toss it—it wasn't even hers. So, in desperation, she said aloud, "God, I give this to You. I don't know what to do."

Moments later, a man approached her and said, "Lady, do you want your umbrella fixed?" He turned out to be an umbrella mender. While she visited her hosts, he repaired the umbrella. Problem solved. That's what happens when you release the problem—you make room for unexpected solutions.

Whenever you make a denial—refuse to accept an undesirable condition—follow it with a strong affirmation of truth.

I once received a call in the middle of the night. A man I had never met was very ill. I denied the reality of disease and affirmed instead: "This man is a perfect idea in Divine Mind, pure substance expressing health and perfection." Distance didn't matter. The result was immediate. That's the power of thought aligned with truth—it travels instantly, and it does not return void.

People often ask me the difference between visualizing and visioning. Visualizing is a mental process—you try to picture something in your mind through effort. Visioning, on the other hand, comes from the higher self. It's intuitive. It's a download, not a creation.

You don't have to push or force anything into existence. Ask: "What does God want for me?" The old, ego-based desires fade, and a better blueprint—your divine blueprint—emerges. And that blueprint always includes the full square of life: health, wealth, love, and right purpose.

A student once told me she needed $100 the next day to pay a crucial debt. I declared that God is never late, and the money was already hers. That evening, she felt nudged to check her safe deposit box—something she hadn't done in ages. At the bottom was a brand-new $100 bill. She swore she had never seen it before. Perhaps it was a materialization. Either way, the supply arrived—on time.

When you align with the divine and speak with the authority of your higher self, the impossible becomes normal. Jesus materialized loaves and fishes. We, too, are meant to live in the miraculous.

There is real power in invoking the name "Jesus Christ," because it represents Truth made manifest. It shifts you into the higher dimension, where you're untouched by fear, illusion, and outside influence. It aligns you with your highest potential—the divine spark within you that never gets sick, never fails, never fears.

We each carry the Christ within—our true, perfect self. This is the aspect of us that was never born and will never die. This is the version of us that can manifest health, love, abundance, and purpose without limit.

When you think, think as an artist. Be deliberate. Paint your inner canvas with clarity, strength, and joy. Trust that no outside power can distort what you envision with truth and faith.

Right thinking is the way you bring heaven to earth. It's not a metaphor—it's the real goal of this whole game we're playing.

The core principles are simple:

Fearless faith. Nonresistance. Love.

May every reader be released—right now—from whatever has chained them for generations. Whatever has stood between you and your good... let it dissolve.

Know this: the truth sets you free.

Free to fulfill your calling.

Free to step into the divine blueprint of your life—complete with health, wealth, love, and powerful self-expression.

"Be transformed by the renewal of your mind."

Modern Affirmations for Daily Practice

For Prosperity

God is my unfailing source.

Money flows to me now in large, unexpected ways—quickly, effortlessly, and in alignment with divine order.

For Alignment and Clarity

Anything not designed by Infinite Intelligence is now dissolved.

Only the divine plan takes form in my life.

For Oneness

Only what's true of God is true of me.

I am one with the Creator, and the Creator is one with me.

For Faith

I am one with my good, because I am one with God.

God is both the source and the substance—there is no separation between the Giver and the Gift.

For Clearing Negative Patterns

Divine Love now clears every limiting belief, every wrong pattern, every false condition in my mind, body, and life.

Love is the highest force in existence, and it neutralizes everything unlike itself.

For Health and Healing

Divine Love energizes every cell in my body.
I am filled with light, vitality, and perfect health.
For Clear Vision
My eyes are the eyes of Spirit.
I see with clarity, truth, and divine perspective.
My path is open and guided.
For Inner Guidance
I am tuned into divine wisdom.
I follow intuitive direction instantly and with trust.
For Hearing Truth
My ears hear only truth, love, and joy.
I am open, receptive, and ready to be led to greater good.
For Right Work & Purpose
I do meaningful work, in the right way, at the right time.
I give with excellence, and I am paid with abundance.